THE HINDU VISION

THE HINDU VISION

ANANTANAND RAMBACHAN

MOTILAL BANARSIDASS PUBLISHERS
PRIVATE LIMITED ● DELHI

First Edition: Delhi, 1992
Reprint: Delhi, 1994, 1999

ISBN: 81-208-1059-7

Also available at:

MOTILAL BANARSIDASS

41 U.A. Bungalow Road, Jawahar Nagar, Delhi 110 007
8 Mahalaxmi Chamber, Warden Road, Mumbai 400 026
120 Royapettah High Road, Mylapore, Chennai 600 004
Sanas Plaza, 1302, Baji Rao Road, Pune 411 002
16 St. Mark's Road, Bangalore 560 001
8 Camac Street, Calcutta 700 017
Ashok Rajpath, Patna 800 004
Chowk, Varanasi 221 001

PRINTED IN INDIA
BY JAINENDRA PRAKASH JAIN AT SHRI JAINENDRA PRESS,
A-45 NARAINA, PHASE I, NEW DELHI 110 028
AND PUBLISHED BY NARENDRA PRAKASH JAIN FOR
MOTILAL BANARSIDASS PUBLISHERS PRIVATE LIMITED,
BUNGALOW ROAD, DELHI 110 007

for Geeta

Contents

Preface

During the years 1983-86, I was invited, on various occasions, by the British Broadcasting Corporation to record a series of talks on Hinduism. These lectures were transmitted around the world on the radio series entitled, "Reflections." Twenty-one talks, each just under five minutes in length, were broadcasted during this period. The topics were diverse and included discussions of Hindu worship, the goals of Hindu life, a Hindu view of Jesus, death and dying in Hinduism, and the spirituality of action in the *Bhagavadgītā*.

Several friends have prompted me to make these talks available in book-form, and it is with their encouragement these are offered here. Amendments have been made to the lectures for the purpose of publication, but I have attempted to preserve the conversational tone with which they were originally delivered. Speaking about Hinduism requires selectivity and generalization and the material presented here reflects the deep influence of the *Vedānta*, and particularly the *Advaita*, tradition on my understanding of Hinduism.

I am deeply grateful to Pauline Webb of the British Broadcasting Corporation who invited me to deliver these lectures and who patiently taught me my first lessons in radio broadcasting. I am thankful to Dr. Jon Moline, the Dean of Saint Olaf College, who generously supported the preparation of this manuscript, and Brett Rabe and Craig Rice who undertook the typing and formatting. I am indebted to my wife, Geeta, who assisted in various ways with the original broadcasts and who has been a source of encouragement and valuable suggestions. Finally, I wish to record my appreciation to the many BBC listeners who responded with questions and letters of encouragement.

Chapter 1

Worship in Hinduism

Diversity is perhaps the first and most important feature of Hindu worship to be noted. The term *"Hindu"* was used originally to describe a geographical entity rather than a uniform religious culture. Today, it refers to a multiplicity of beliefs and practices. Given the close connection between Hinduism and the land of India, this diversity is not inexplicable. It reflects the astonishing variation in geography, language, and culture across the Indian sub-continent. Each region has contributed its favorite deities and its distinctive customs and rituals into the melting pot of the Hindu tradition. The history of Hinduism therefore, is the record of what has gone on in the regions of India, and is the result of this long process of interaction and absorption. This tendency to assimilate has become a characteristic feature of Hinduism, and one which is enthusiastically defended by its apologists.

> When conceived in a large historical spirit, Hinduism becomes a slow growth across the centuries incorporating all the good and true things as well as much that is evil and erroneous, though

> a constant endeavour, which is not always successful, is kept up to throw out the unsatisfactory elements .... It allows each group to get to the truth through its own tradition by means of discipline of mind and morals. Each group has its own historic tradition, and assimilation of it is the condition of its growth of spirit.[1]

This diversity, however, has been counterbalanced by a certain uniformity derived from the Sanskrit tradition rooted in the prestigious literature of the *Vedas*. It has added a coherence through common myths, customs, values, and concepts. Contemporary Hinduism reveals a dynamic interaction of various regional traditions with this embracing Sanskrit tradition, and the domination of one or the other varies.

For some of the reasons already mentioned, Hindu worship presents a rich variety of content and forms, often bewildering to the outside observer. It includes rituals and ceremonies of great complexity and details of procedure, to the most simple, informal, and spontaneous. All these specific forms of worship, however, have one common aim in which they are fulfilled. The aim is through particular acts of worship, at special times and places, to make of one's whole life a continuous act of worship.

Before describing some of the ways in which we worship, it will be useful to discuss some of the implicit and often unspoken attitudes which we bring to our worship. An understanding of these will help to reduce the bewilderment which our worship can quite easily invoke. Much of the variety of Hindu worship is the result of the concept of the *iṣṭadeva*, or the deity of one's choice. This concept is partly the result of the plurality of the environment in which Hinduism developed, and the recognition of the diversity of human personalities. It is a view which also helps to explain a certain liberality of outlook in Hinduism towards other religions. Within a certain framework, we have the freedom to choose concepts and representations of God with which we can most easily identify, and with whom we can enter into a relationship. Among the most popular chosen deities are the various incarnations or *avatāras* of God. In the *Bhagavadgītā*, we are told that God incarnates from time to time to revitalize the search for righteousness and ultimate spiritual values. The incarnations of Rāma and Kṛṣṇa are perhaps the two most popular *iṣṭadevas* or deities chosen for personal worship by Hindus. The reasons for a particular choice are many. The deity might have been traditionally worshipped in the family or the individual may be attracted to certain features and attributes of the deity. Many of us, for example, find it more appropriate to conceive of the creator and sustainer of the universe through the symbols of femininity and motherhood. There are also, therefore, many female representations of God in Hinduism worshipped as the mother of the universe. It is not uncommon to find the members of any Hindu home choosing different personal deities for worship.

There are many reasons why this plurality of representations of God is not, for us, confusing or conflicting. Each chosen deity is completely identified with the qualities and attributes of Godhead, such as omnipotence and omniscience, and is not opposed to another similar representation. The unity and oneness of God is most strongly affirmed side by side with this multiplicity of representation in worship. The guiding principle for us is the *Ṛg Veda* text, "Truth is one; it is spoken of diversely." There is also a very beautiful and often quoted verse of the *Bhagavadgītā* in which Kṛṣṇa says: "In whatsoever ways people approach me, in that same way do I return their love; for the paths people take from every side are Mine." (4:11)

As I have already mentioned, there are many reasons why we might choose a particular deity for worship. Our choice could be influenced by the nature of the relationship which we wish to have with God. In our worship, some kinds of relationships are common. We refer to the first of these as *dāsya bhāva.* Here, the worshipper conceives of God as master and of herself as servant. A more intimate and preferable relationship for many of us is *sakhya bhāva.* God is viewed as a personal friend, always near, and to whom one's heart can be open. He is a comrade on the journey of life. Many of our mothers choose to worship God as child. This attitude is known as *vātsalya bhāva.* The baby Kṛṣṇa, for example, evokes maternal love and adoration, and Hindu mothers find it easy to identify with the mothers of Rāma and Kṛṣṇa. This attitude is understandable among religions which share a doctrine of the incarnation of God. It is a form of worship which can be observed especially on the occasions when the births of our incarnations are celebrated. Conversely, one may choose to think of oneself as child, and of God as mother or father. Perhaps the most intense and close relationship in our tradition is *madhura bhāva,* where God is thought of as a husband and the worshipper as wife. He is the eternal beloved. These relationships are, of course, not exclusive, and one may at different times adopt different attitudes.

Another important feature of our worship is the profuse use of various symbols and images, or what we refer to as *mūrtis.* The place of these in our worship has often brought and still brings upon us the accusation of idolatry. Some words of explanation, therefore are necessary. Diana Eck points to an important reason for this historical distrust.

> On the whole, it would be fair to say that the Western traditions, especially the religious traditions of the "Book"— Judaism, Christianity, and Islam — have trusted the Word more than the Im-

> age as a mediator of the divine truth. The Qur'an and the Hebrew Bible are filled with injunctions to "proclaim" and to "hear" the word. The ears were somehow more trustworthy than the eyes.[2]

In surveying our attitudes about images, two principal approaches can be distinguished. In the first approach, the *mūrti* is viewed as a symbolic focus for concentration and worship. The symbolic nature of the *mūrti* is often cited in defense of its use. The Hindu scholar, Satischandra Chatterjee writes:

> It is a mistake to think that the worship of images, approved by Hinduism, is crude idolatry. For image-worship is really the worship of God as represented by means of images. These images by themselves are neither looked upon as God nor worshipped as such. They are treated only as symbols or concrete representations of God.[3]

In the second approach, the *mūrti* is perceived as a real embodiment of God and not merely a symbolic focus for concentration or worship. It is an actual manifestation of God. This view has been particularly elaborated by the Śrī Vaiṣṇava community through its most distinguished theologian, Rāmānuja, in the eleventh century. The image is understood as one of the five ways in which the Lord manifests Himself. In the supreme (*para*) form, the Lord eternally abides in heaven. The emanations (*vyūha*) of the Lord preside over the functions of creation, preservation, and destruction. At specific times, the Lord manifests (*vibhava*) or incarnates. Divine personalities like Rāma and Kṛṣṇa represent such earthly incarnations (*avatāras*). The Lord resides in the heart of all human beings as the inner controller (*antaryāmin*). Finally, and most important for the Śrī Vaiṣṇavas, is the descent of the Lord into the world as an image. The term *arcāvatāra* is used to refer to this "image incarnation."[4] It is a form in which the Lord makes Himself accessible for worship.

The Hindu acceptance of the *arcāvatāra* concept has to be understood in the context of its prevalent views about the nature of God and His relationship to the world. According to Rāmānuja, God is the only reality. There is no existence outside or independent of God. God, however, contains within Himself the world of individual souls and material objects. Within the all-inclusive God exist unconscious matter and finite spirits. Rāmānuja uses the analogy of body and soul for clarifying the relationship between the Lord and the universe. Matter and souls are conceived of as constituting the body of God. God, as the soul of the entire universe, pervades, controls, guides and uses it as an instrument. For the Advaita philosopher, Śaṅkara, the entire universe is an inexplicable appearance of God who is both its intelligent and material cause. In either view, the universe as a whole and all its particular forms are pervaded by God. All forms belong to God and each can serve as a medium for appreciating and worshipping Him. The fact that the axis of the universe literally runs through everything, grants to all objects the potential for revealing God.

The persistent equation of the *arcāvatāra* concept with idolatry ought also to be examined in the light of the clear and strong affirmation of divine transcendence in Hinduism. We have already noted that in Vaiṣṇava theology, the *arcā* form is only one of the five ways in which the Lord is understood to manifest Himself. The Hindu concept of God as both immanent in the world and transcendent over it is expressed figuratively in the *Vedas* in the view that God pervades the world by a fourth of his being, while three-fourths of him remain beyond it. The *Bhagavadgītā* similarly affirms that while the entire universe owes its being to God, the forms of the universe do not contain or express him fully (9:4-5). It is clearly recognized that no finite process or form can ever finally express the absolute. Ultimately, however, we appreciate the limitations of all our concepts and forms of worship. This is movingly expressed in a traditional Hindu prayer for forgiveness:

> In my meditations, I have attributed forms to You who transcend all forms.
> By my songs of praise, I have contradicted that you are indescribable.
> By my pilgrimage, I have denied your omnipresence.
> O Lord of the universe, forgive me these limitations.

We have just discussed the different relationships which we can choose to have with God, and the significance of the use of *mūrtis* in our worship. I now wish to describe some of the worship practices in our homes.

For most of us, the home is the important center of religious life and worship, and the place where we gather our primary knowledge of spiritual values and practices. We are not constrained by any obligation to worship in temples, and there are many of us who seldom visit temples. Congregational worship, as generally understood, is not a significant feature of Hindu worship. The individual nature of worship largely prevails.

The term, *pūjā*, which literally means worship, is used to describe the various forms of worship in the home or in the temple. A *pūjā* is an act of reverence by a devotee towards a chosen representation of God, indicated by the presence of the *mūrti*. Strictly speaking, a *pūjā* is a formal mode of worship with its conventionally prescribed procedures or *upacāras* venerating the Lord as an honoured guest. The procedures are generally about fourteen in number. Among the important procedures of a *pūjā* are the initial invocation of the deity (*āvāhana*), the invitation to a seat (*āsana*), the washing of the feet (*pādya*), and acts of adoration through the offering of flowers, the burning of incense, the waving of lights (*dīpa*) and the consecration of food (*naivedya*). These acts are accompanied by the recitation of appropriate scriptural texts and forms of meditation. The *pūjā* ritual concludes with the distribution of *prasāda*, that is, food which has been ritually offered to the deity. The acceptance of *prasāda* is an acknowledgement of the Lord as the source of all that we enjoy. The word also means grace, and is symbolic of the blessings of the deity. A *pūjā*, therefore, is a total involvement of the body, speech, and mind in worship.

Most Hindu homes have a special room or corner of another room set aside for the purpose of worship. On a shrine will be kept the *mūrtis* of the family *iṣṭadevas*, that is the chosen deities, or perhaps some utensils for worship. This section of each home has an atmosphere of special sanctity and is the focus of family devotion. Great care is taken to maintain its cleanliness and purity.

There is great variation in the forms of worship in our homes, depending on factors such as individual competence, general family circumstances, or even personal preferences. In some homes, for example, there will be the full *pūjā* ritual performed daily by a competent family member or a priest appointed for this purpose. In most homes, however, the entire *pūjā* ritual will only be conducted a few times each year. Daily worship, therefore, generally takes the form of a few selected procedures from the *pūjā* ceremony. These are usually performed twice daily, on mornings and evenings. It is important to note that the initiative and leading role in family worship is commonly undertaken by the Hindu mother who plays a very important role in the transmission of our religious tradition.

The presence of a properly consecrated and installed *mūrti* literally transforms the family home into an abode of the Lord. It becomes a sacred environment in which all aspects of life are centered and focused on God. For the Hindu, the *mūrti* is a potent reminder of God's eternal presence and His existence in all things. It calls us to act as if we are always in the presence of the divine. For one whose consciousness is so imbued with a sense of the divine, God cannot be ignored. In his *arca* form he is the beloved household guest, around whom all activities revolve and to whom everything is dedicated.

Perhaps the most common form of worship in our homes is the daily performance of the *āratī* ceremony. This is the waving of a flame of light before the *mūrti* in a clockwise direction. Each family member may perform the ritual or it may be done by one person. The flame is then passed on to the others who receive the blessings of God by holding their hands over the flame and then touching their eyes and foreheads. The *āratī* is essentially a ceremony of loving adoration and reverence, and light is one of the central positive symbols of Hinduism.

Āratī is usually accompanied by the recitation of scriptural verses (*mantras*) or the singing of hymns (*bhajana*). One of the verses recited comes from the *Kaṭha Upaniṣad* and is one of my favourite texts. It most beautifully expresses the paradox of trying to illumine the Lord with a tiny, flickering flame. The following is a translation of the Sanskrit text:

> You are not illumined by the splendor of the sun,
> the moon, the stars, or even the bright flashes
> of lightning. Of what avail then is this tiny

flame?
It is after You that all of these shine, and through Your lustre that they were illumined. (*Kaṭha Upaniṣad* 2.2. 15)

Another common form of worship in our homes is the singing of *bhajanas* or *kīrtana*. Both can be done at the time of the *āratī* ceremony or be a separate form of worship. A *bhajana* is a song of devotion. Many date back to the medieval period of Indian history which witnessed a great flowering of the devotional movement. Songs by saintly composers of that time like Kabir, Surdas, Tulsidas, and the female singer Mira are daily sung in Hindu homes. Most of the themes of these songs center around the incarnations of Rāma and Kṛṣṇa. They describe the attributes of the Lord and the compassionate nature of His activities. Many of these relate to the Lord as the irresistible and attractive beloved, and express an intense yearning for his vision (*darśana*). A *kīrtana*, on the other hand, is a musical recitation of the various names of God. Each name defines an essential quality of God, and several such names are combined and sung repeatedly. Again, these center primarily on the figures of Rāma and Kṛṣṇa and constitute a form of contemplation on the nature of God. Both forms of worship are generally accompanied by music, which plays an important role in Hindu worship.

In describing our worship practices, it is important to note that all of the sacraments (*saṃskāras*) marking important stages in the life of the individual are performed in the home. Among the most important of such rites are those concerned with the birth of a child, initiation into religious life, marriage, and death. All of these are essentially religious in nature and are very important occasions of family worship.

Having discussed the Hindu home as the center of daily worship, we shall now briefly consider the significance of the

Hindu temple as a place of worship.

Hindu temples vary in both size and shape. One will find large, extraordinary beautiful temples, as well as small and simple ones standing humbly at village roadsides. Whether small or large, however, they all share a common feature. The Hindu temple is conceived primarily as the abode of the particular deity to whom it is dedicated. Temples may be dedicated to any one of the many Hindu deities. The central feature of any Hindu temple, therefore, is the *garbhagṛha* (inner sanctuary) where the particular form of the deity has been ritually installed. The inner shrine is covered by a pyramidal canopy or roof, the function of which is to denote honor and eminence. Traditionally, Hindu temples were not constructed to accommodate congregational prayer, and were meant primarily for individual worship. It is interesting to note, however, that the temples constructed by Hindus who have settled outside of India are designed for forms of congregational worship and also serve wider functions.

Larger Hindu temples have a priest or a group of priests whose responsibility is to care for the deity and to conduct the regular daily schedule of worship. Generally speaking, daily worship in the Hindu temple is based on the concept of God as king of kings. Worship begins in the silent dawn when the deity is symbolically roused from sleep with soft, solemn music and the recitation of scriptural verses. The awakening ceremony is followed by the ceremonial bath, after which the deity is annointed with sandal paste, dressed in royal robes and decked with ornaments and flowers. Hymns and prayers are recited during the day and there are regular offerings of food for consecration. Worship ends with an elaborate *ārati* ritual. On special festive occasions the deity is taken out in procession.

For us, the primary purpose of visiting a temple is to have *darśana* of the deity. The concept of *darśana* in our tradition is a very rich one. It means more than the physical sight of the deity. It is to enter from the mundane into the presence, atmosphere, and awe of the sacred. The mind is lifted, however temporarily, into an awareness of a deeper reality and significance of life. At the temple, we also make offerings of fruits and flowers in thankfulness for the bounties of the Lord, or as an accompaniment to our prayerful requests. No visit to a Hindu temple is complete without the receiving of *prasāda*, representative of the grace of God.

The Hindu scriptures are not unaware of the dangers of overdoing this kind of worship. Such worship is considered to be preliminary and not the ultimate aim of religious life. We aim through acts such as these to cultivate an unbroken awareness of God. This is the goal held out by Kṛṣṇa in the *Bhagavadgītā*:

> One who sees Me everywhere and sees everything in Me,
> of him I shall never lose hold and he shall never lose hold of Me (6:30)

In our discussion so far, we have concerned ourselves with the significance of the deities in worship, the purpose of *mūrtis*, and some of the forms of worship in our homes and temples. Other important occasions of worship are associated with the many festivals of our tradition. Some of these are seasonal, some celebrate the harvest or fertility of the fields, while others commemorate the births of incarnations like Rāma and Kṛṣṇa. In concluding, I have chosen to return to a theme which I was only able to hint at in the beginning of this discussion. I think it is fitting to emphasize here the aim of Hindu worship to make living itself an act of worship.

While we ascribe great importance to all forms of worship which I have described, the hope is always to overcome the identification of worship with distinct actions performed only at certain times and places. The intention is to rise above the division between the religious and non-religious dimensions of life. If worship is the highest and most joyful activity we engage in, then the aim must certainly be to make it continuous. Hindu worship, then, finds its culmination when we discover the beauty of offering every one of our actions to God, and living itself becomes synonymous with the joy of worship. This supreme ideal of making life itself worship is one of the central themes of Kṛṣṇa in the *Bhagavadgītā*:

> Whatever you do, whatever you eat, whatever you offer in sacrifice or give away in alms, whatever penance you may perform, offer it up to Me. (9:27)

This aspiration is also voiced in a well-known prayer which we recite in Sanskrit at the conclusion of any specific worship. The following is a translation of this prayer:

> I offer unto God all of the actions which, according to their respective capacities and natures, I perform through my body, senses, mind, and intellect.

As our creator, we recognize that our relationship with God, unlike many of our day to day relationships, is not one that we can temporarily assume during worship and then discard with a change of time and place. Being the most fundamental, it ought to be continuous and unbroken, informing and determining all other relationships and activities. For us, the way to preserving the attitude of worship in all of our activites is given in an important *Bhagavadgītā* verse:

> To action alone you have the right and never at all to its fruits; let not the fruits of action be your motive; neither let there be in you any attachment to inaction. (2:47)

We understand this verse to suggest that as human beings we can and must always act. The results of our actions, however, are ultimately determined by God. We try to learn, therefore, to cheerfully accept the results, pleasant or unpleasant, as coming from Him. Our attitude to these is the same as when we accept *prasāda*, that is food offered to the deity at the end of worship in the home or temple. Dedication of the action to God is done once the fruit of action is gladly accepted with all reverence as His *prasāda* or blessing.

NOTES

1. S. Radhakrishnan, *The Hindu View Of Life* (London: Unwin Paperbacks, 1980), p. 31.

2. D. Eck, *Darśan, Seeing the Divine Image in India* (Pennsylvania: Anima Books, 1985), p. 20.

3. S. Chatterjee, *The Fundamentals of Hinduism* (Calcutta: The University of Calcutta, 1970), pp. 176-77.

4. Vasudha Narayanan, "Arcāvatāra: On Earth as He is in Heaven," in Joanne Punzo Waghorne and Norman Cutler eds., *Gods of Flesh/Gods of Stone* (Pennsylvania: Anima Publications, 1985), pp. 53-68.

Chapter 2

Fullness of Life in Hinduism

The term "Hinduism" shelters a great diversity of beliefs and practices. The Persians who invaded India through the North-Western passes of the Himalayas referred to the districts near the river Sindhu as, "Hindu." The term, therefore, originally described a geographical area rather than a uniform system of beliefs and practices. That diversity, which must have originally been there, is still with us today. Like a large, many-branched, very ancient family, there are underlying unifying factors, but also a considerable diversity of beliefs and practices. While all of us, for example, would accept *mokṣa*, that is, spiritual freedom, as the ultimate goal of life, there would be different shades of opinion about its nature and means of accomplishment. This would also apply to other matters of doctrine.

With this wealth of diversity in mind, I shall focus this discussion on the four goals or possibilities which Hinduism sees as constituting the full human life. While it is necessary to discuss these goals in some order or sequence, one should not expect that their fulfillment also proceeds in a similar sequence. The ideal is a simultaneous pursuit and realization of all four ends and the achievement of harmony and balance among them. They are together seen as essential to the perfecting and realizing of the full potential of the human person. The first component of the full human life is referred to, in Sanskrit, as *artha.* The term *artha* is very broad in its meaning and is generally equated with wealth. By presenting *artha* as one of the goals of life, Hinduism recognizes that every human being has certain basic material wants such as the need for food, clothing, and shelter, and it is legitimate that these be fulfilled. The obvious lack of these necessities in certain parts of the Indian sub-continent should not be interpreted to mean that Hinduism has given its blessings to involuntary poverty. In spite of appearances to the contrary, the spirituality of Hinduism is not anti-materialistic.

In addition to requiring certain material necessities for decent living, we also possess the capacity for pleasure and enjoyment through our senses. It is this pleasure, referred to, in Sanskrit, as *kāma,* which constitutes the second component of the fully realized human life. *Kāma* includes both sensual and aesthetic pleasure. Sculpture, music, and dance grew and flourished with the blessings of Hinduism, and Hindus love to celebrate life through these forms. *Kāma* legitimizes the human need and capacity for pleasure; the necessities of life are to be enjoyed as a way of fulfilling human nature.

Because Hinduism is often characterized as life-denying and other-worldly, it might surprise one to learn that wealth and pleasure are two of the legitimate components of life. It is true that Hinduism does not uphold these as the highest ends or values, but Hindus are not so spiritually minded that they despise material things.

The pursuit of wealth and pleasure, however, does not make us unique as a species of living beings. Other forms of life also require certain basic physical necessities and are capable of varying degrees of sensual and mental pleasures. It is the third component of life termed, in Sanskrit, as *dharma*, which, in the first instance, distinguishes us as human beings.

Dharma is a very rich and multi-faceted concept within the Hindu tradition and therefore, difficult to translate into the English language. The word is derived from a Sanskrit root meaning to support or maintain, and can be partly equated with virtue or righteousness. The human being is not only capable of pursuing wealth and pleasure, but is capable of virtue as well. *Dharma* emphasizes the social context in which we aspire after wealth and pleasure. Through *dharma*, we are reminded that the selfish and uncontrolled pursuit of wealth and pleasure lead to social chaos and disharmony. *Dharma* demands that we broaden our perspective to incorporate the good and welfare of the society as a whole. The personal attainment of wealth and pleasure by inflicting pain and suffering on others, or by denying them the right to freely pursue these two ends is opposed to *dharma*.

Dharma is the principle in Hinduism which presupposes the unique human capacity for concern and responsiveness towards the needs and interests of others. It seeks to remind us that our rights as individuals are only possible and meaningful in a context where equal, if not greater, recognition is given to our duties and obligations. We are the only animal species with the capacity to make conscious moral choices in relation to our wealth and pleasure oriented activities. Being human requires that we continuously exercise this choice.

While emphasizing *dharma* as a fundamental component of human life, the Hindu tradition does not minimize the difficulty of determining the right course of action in a specific situation. A Hindu scriptural text, the *Mahābhārata*, for example, tells the story of a monk who was so faithful in telling the truth that he was known as the truth-teller. One day, a group of thieves who were hotly pursuing some terrified travelers, knowing the monk's reputation, asked him where the travelers had gone. The monk truthfully pointed out the route they had taken, and, with his help, the thieves were able to slay and rob the travelers. The text condemns the monk for selfishly ignoring the subtleties of *dharma*. While speech should be true, the end result ought to be beneficial.

In Hindu mythology, the symbol of *dharma* is the bull, whose four feet are truth (*satya*), purity (*śauca*), compassion (*dayā*), and charity (*dāna*). While there is no infallible way of determining *dharma*, a pure mind, intent on truth and blessed with compassion and charity is the most reliable guide in our quest for it.

As an end which is founded upon human freedom, choice, and responsibility, responsiveness to the demands of *dharma* is highly valued within the Hindu tradition. Now that I have mentioned freedom and choice, I have reached a good point in this discussion to explore one of the difficult and often misunderstood concepts of Hinduism. I am referring here to the doctrine of *karma*. After considering this, I will look at the meaning of spiritual freedom, that is, *mokṣa*, which is the ultimate goal of life in Hinduism.

The word *karma* literally means action. When, however, we Hindus speak of *karma* as a basic doctrine of Hinduism, we imply that all actions are governed by a certain law. The nature of this law is perhaps best understood by looking at it in relation to a view which is accepted without question. As far as actions in our physical world are concerned, we agree that there can be no event or effect without a cause. We also agree that any action will produce an effect which is determined by the nature of the effect or cause. The distance which an arrow travels through the air, for example, is determined by the force with which it is released from its bow. In general, however, we limit our understanding of the relationship between causes and effects only to the physical aspect of actions. We may not be as willing to accept that moral actions are as forceful as physical actions and are also capable of producing consequences like happiness or misery, joys and sorrows. This, however, is exactly the point which Hinduism seeks to affirm through the law of *karma*. It is an extension of our understanding of causation to the sphere of moral actions and results.

In a simple way, Hindus understand that law of *karma* to mean that all actions which we perform, good or bad, will produce their appropriate results, at some stage, in our lives. Through the law of *karma*, we view the world as a moral stage, and see ourselves as being under the judgement of a moral law.

In the Hindu understanding, however, the moral consequences of our actions may not always be apparent during the course of the same life in which the actions are performed. In Hinduism, we understand the soul or spirit to be uncreated and beginningless. Life is a pilgrimage, a journey of experience and learning, through many different births towards the freedom of spiritual liberation. Even as birth, for us, is not an absolute beginning, death does not mean complete extinction. Birth implies the association of the soul with a new body, while death implies the dissociation from that body. This journey through a continuous and connected series of life experiences towards freedom is governed by the law of *karma* or moral causation.

Within the framework of this view therefore, we can readily accept that our actions in the present could produce results for us in a subsequent life experience. It also follows, for us, that some of our present experiences can only be explained by actions and events in previous life occurrences.

The doctrine of *karma* is often understood to be denying freedom of will and choice for the human being. It is argued that we lose all initiative and responsibility for actions if our experiences in the present life are determined by our actions in the past. Many Hindus themselves cite the doctrine of *karma* to justify an attitude of fatalistic resignation and indifference to the circumstances of their lives in societies.

Properly understood, however, the law of *karma* emphasizes free will and insists upon moral responsibility. If in my present life I am experiencing the results and consequences of my past actions, this is only because I was responsible for these actions. The important point, of course, is that if I have influenced my present condition through my past behavior, there is no reason why I should not be able to shape my future through my present conduct. The law of *karma* stipulates that certain kinds of actions will naturally produce certain results, but this does not thereby paralyze our wills. On the contrary, it places responsibility squarely on our shoulders since it does not propose a power outside of ourselves which is responsible for our individual and collective destinies.

We must, at the same time, admit that the effects of certain past actions could be difficult to overcome or alter. There is, however, nothing mysterious about this, since it is true of any habit of thinking or acting developed over a long period of time. It only means that powerful and undesirable past ways of thinking and acting require greater efforts of will to transcend and overcome them.

For most Hindus, the law of *karma* is believed to be under the guidance and control of God. As a law which makes for justice and righteousness, it expresses God's moral nature in the order of the universe. The doctrine of *karma* does not negate or exclude God's compassion or forgiveness. God's compassion, however, also requires of us the responses of repentance and purification and can be seen therefore, as being within the context of *karma.*

Before concluding my discussion of this doctrine, I would like to respond to another unfortunate misunderstanding of its implications. It is often argued that *karma* discourages efforts to relieve the suffering of others since misery is viewed as the just reward of undesirable actions in the past. It must always be remembered, however, that the Hindu tradition which proposes *karma*, also requires us to respond continuously with compassion and charity, that is *dayā* and *dāna*, towards all beings. If some of our fellow beings suffer because of sinful actions in the past, it is also wrong of us in the present not to try, as best as we can, to relieve and comfort them in their suffering. To justify our indifference by appealing to the doctrine of *karma* is a sad and pitiable way of shirking our duty to care for our fellow beings.

In my discussion, so far, I have considered three of the four components of the full human life as understood in Hinduism. These are wealth (*artha*), pleasure (*kāma*), and virtue or righteousness (*dharma*). In spite of the high value placed upon *dharma* and the necessity and difficulty of living up to its demands, it is not, along with wealth and pleasure, considered to be the highest end of human life. In other words, a life which consisted of the search for wealth and pleasure within the framework of the moral obligations of *dharma* does not exhaust the highest possibilities of the human being. The Sanskrit term *mokṣa*, which means freedom, describes the highest end of life in Hinduism.

We do not, however, come to this goal of life very easily. The urge for wealth and pleasure is quite common; the appreciation of the value of *dharma* is less commonly found. The desire for *mokṣa* is the rarest of them all. It comes when in spite of fulfilling desire after desire for wealth and pleasure, we feel a deep want and lack within us which ever remains unfulfilled. It comes when we somehow feel that as important as our material wants are, satisfying these cannot be the ultimate purpose of our lives. At that moment when we feel the need to know whether there is any deeper significance to life, the quest for *mokṣa* really begins.

The term *mokṣa*, as already mentioned, means freedom. Freedom, however, is always from something, and *mokṣa* primarily means freedom from ignorance. In Sanskrit, this ignorance is called, *avidyā*. Whereas the Christian tradition, for example, affirms the idea of an original sin to which we are all subject, Hinduism speaks of a beginningless ignorance which blinds us all. This ignorance is about ourselves, about who we are, and *mokṣa* is freedom from this.

A traditional story is used by Hindu teachers to illustrate the nature of our self-ignorance. The story tells of ten disciples who went out walking in the woods. Along the way, they encountered a river which was in flood. They thought it would be good fun to swim across and all entered the swift-flowing water. When they reached the opposite bank, the leader wanted to ensure that his brother-disciples were safe. He took a quick count, and, to his great dismay, found that only nine were present. There was great anxiety and uproar as each, in turn, counted and found only nine. A woodcutter who was working nearby heard their noises and inquired about the problem. They explained the cause of their sorrow and he himself took a quick count. "Do not worry," he assured them, "I will find the tenth man for you." He then asked the leader to check their numbers again, but he could still only find nine. "What about yourself?", inquired the woodcutter, with a smile. "You are the tenth man!" They all immediately saw their error; they had always omitted themselves from the count. The tenth man was only lost in their ignorance. Our ignorance about ourselves, affirms Hinduism, is not different from that of the so-called missing tenth man.

Hinduism sees this problem of self-ignorance as a fundamental one, since our behavior and responses to other human beings are largely determined by what we perceive or do not perceive ourselves to be.

What is it about ourselves that Hinduism says we do not know? This question is best answered by looking first at what we seek in life. Hinduism affirms that we all naturally seek fullness and wish to avoid sorrow and unhappiness. We generally try to do this by increasing enjoyment through our senses and by multiplying our needs and possessions. We become selfish competitors with every other being in our private quest for happiness. Is our search for fullness, Hinduism asks, only through sense enjoyment and material possessions valid? Can these ever fully satisfy us? Hinduism's answer to both questions is negative. We will be disappointed and disillusioned if we make these ends the sole concerns of our lives.

Self-ignorance consists of the fact that we take ourselves to be identical with the physical body which is subject to birth, change, decline, and eventually death. We are not even the mind, Hinduism tells us, composed of a variety and succession of thoughts, moods, and feelings. The essential nature of every being is distinct from the body and mind. The term used for the Self or being of every living thing is *ātman*. Unlike the body, the *ātman* is immortal. It is never born, nor will it ever die. Unlike the mind, it is not subject to change. The *ātman* is equally and identically present in all beings. Contrary to the notion we have of ourselves as distinct and separate from every other being, we are united in the *ātman* which is identical in each of us. It is free, full, and complete and it is the truth and reality of our natures. It is this knowledge of the *ātman* which constitutes *mokṣa* in Hinduism.

Mokṣa is freedom from self-ignorance, but what are

we to use this freedom for? Hinduism conceives of a life where human beings can live out of the fullness and joy of the *ātman*. Existence can become a celebration in its most profound sense. Instead of searching through acquisitions of every imaginable kind for a fullness which ever evades us, we are called upon to discover and live from a fullness with which we are already blessed. *Mokṣa* is not a selfish concern with oneself. In fact, it is the exact opposite. Because it tells us of a truth about ourselves which informs us of a unity we share with all beings, it draws us out of the isolated perception of ourselves. *Mokṣa* celebrates the oneness and unity of existence, and provides a profound basis for a life of unselfish activity and giving. The Hindu tradition, unfortunately, has not always been consistent in insisting upon these values as necessary and integral to this vision of oneness and unity. In a world where differences of culture, religion, and nationality are the causes of violence and suffering, we need to be reminded of the fundamental unity of all existence which the Hindu goal of *mokṣa* affirms.

Chapter 3

Understanding Death and Dying in Hinduism

Hinduism recommends five daily sacrifices for all Hindus. These are referred to, in Sanskrit, as the *Pañca Mahāyajña*, that is, the Five Great Sacrifices. The first of these is the *Brahma Yajña*, the pursuit of spiritual enlightenment. This consists of the study and teaching of Hindu scriptural texts. The second is the *Deva Yajña*, the worship of God, and this is fulfilled through daily worship practices. The third is the *Pitṛ Yajña*, the sacrifice for the departed ancestors, which is accomplished by appropriate offerings and prayer for their well being. In a wider sense, service to the elderly is also regarded as included in it. The fourth is the *Manuṣya Yajña*, the sacrifice to human beings, and this consists of feeding, clothing and housing the destitute and homeless. It is a duty to actively alleviate the distress of others. The final is the *Bhūta Yajña*, the sacrifice to non-human life, and this is fulfilled by caring for and meeting the needs of other species. These five daily sacrifices recognize the interconnectedness and interdependence of all life, and by the regular performance of these, the Hindu strives to express a natural gratitude to God, spiritual teachers, ancestors, fellow-beings, and non-human life.

In addition to prescribing the daily performance of the *Pitṛ Yajña*, Hinduism has also dedicated a special fortnight, for the sacrifice to the departed ancestors. This is referred to, in Sanskrit, as the *Pitṛ Pakṣa*. It is a time when we turn our thoughts to the past and regard with loving gratitude those whose labors have made possible the many blessings which we enjoy. We remind ourselves of the immense debt which we owe to the past and are made humble in the realization of our dependence on those who have gone before us. We are reminded of the time when we will pass away and of our responsibilities to hand down an enriched legacy to the future. We should give with much more abundance than we have received.

The ancestral fortnight also compels us to ponder and consider our own mortal natures. While death is a basic feature of existence and while the ability to reflect on death is unique to human beings, we perplexingly ignore its reality. A Hindu scriptural text, the *Mahābhārata*, describes as the greatest wonder of the world, the fact that we rarely think about death in spite of its certainty. Yet, strangely enough, it is often the realization of the certainty of death which lends extraordinary clarity to the meaning of life. It reveals to us the temporary nature of all those things to which we cling so passionately and which we must eventually let go. The burdens of life become lighter with the realization that nothing really belongs to us. The awareness of death can reorient our sense of values to that which is true and ultimate and lasting. Contemplating death, far from being a morbid experience, can be a truly enlightening one.

Since the reality of death raises the most profound

questions about the meaning and significance of life, every religious tradition has its own unique ways and insights for dealing with it and we will consider some of the resources in Hinduism for coping with death and dying.

In its analysis of the human condition, the Hindu tradition strives to be realistic. An important dimension of this realism is the recognition of death as a natural and universal feature of existence. Death is coeval with life. It is not seen as an aberration or abnormality in the stream of living. In the *Bhagavadgītā* (2:27), the Lord incarnated as Kṛṣṇa comforts his disciple Arjuna, by drawing his attention to this truth:

> To one who is born, death is certain, and certain is birth for the one who has died. Therefore, for what is unavoidable, thou shouldest not grieve.

Gautama Buddha, a distinguished child of Hinduism, skillfully helped a woman, who was deeply grieving over the loss of a child, to discover this truth. After patiently listening to the account of her sadness and loss, the Buddha promised to heal her affliction if she would go to the city and return with a mustard seed from any house in which there had never been a death. Greatly elated she set off, and, after a tireless day of questioning every resident, she was unable to fulfill the Buddha's condition. The lesson of the exercise was quickly learnt. She was not alone in grief — death comes to all. The appreciation of death as a natural and inevitable change in the condition of life helps us to discover a poise and tranquillity, for we can begin to understand the limitations of struggling against the unavoidable. We learn to accept features of existence which we cannot change. This attitude of quiet acceptance, however, does not conclude the Hindu understanding of death. It only provides a condition for further inquiry — an inquiry that concerns our view of the human person and indeed of life itself. It is the light of life which makes the meaning of death intelligible.

In the Hindu understanding, the true being or identity of the human person is the Self, or, in Sanskrit, the *ātman*. It is the changeless basis and unifying reality of all other components of the human being. In some Hindu traditions, the *ātman* is identical with God within and outside the individual. Hinduism likens all other elements to sheaths or layers which envelop and clothe the Self. For the purpose of understanding the Hindu attitude to death, two of these sheaths are particularly important. The first is the physical body, visible through the sense organs, and referred to, in Sanskrit, as the *sthūla śarīra*. The second is the subtle body, invisible to the sense organs and composed of the entire inner world of thoughts, feelings, memories, and impressions. It is referred to, in Sanskrit, as the *sūkṣma śarīra*. The change in condition, which we refer to as death, results in the disintegration of the physical body into its constituent elements. This is the only layer of being which is destroyed at death. The Self, clothed with the subtle body, continues the journey of existence, seeking a new physical form in which to express and fulfill its tendencies and desires. Death is the disassociation of the Self with a particular physical form.

Death and birth are gateways of exit and entry to the stage of this world. This process is described in one of the most striking and famous analogies in the entire *Bhagavadgītā* (2:22). It is a text which is movingly recited on the occasion of death and has given comfort and solace to the grieving Hindu heart for centuries:

> Just as a person casts off worn-out garments and puts on others that are new, even so does the embodied-soul cast off worn-out bodies and takes on others that are new.

This analogy is full of suggestions, but I can only briefly draw your attention to a few of these. Firstly, a suit of clothing is not identical with the wearer. Similarly, the physical body, which is likened here to worn-out garments, is not the true being or identity of the human person. Secondly, there is the similarity of a continuity of being. When a worn-out suit of clothing is cast off, the wearer continues to be. Similarly, with the disintegration of the physical body the indweller, that is the Self, continues to be. Finally, there is a parallel with the timing of the change. A suit of clothing is changed when it no longer serves the purpose for which it was intended. Similarly, the physical body is cast off when it no longer serves the purpose for which it came into existence.

Hinduism conceives of life as a continuous chain of existence. Each link in this chain is influenced by the ones preceding it. The physical body, as a vital and necessary component in any particular life experience, is also conditioned by the preceding life occurrences. It is the instrument through which diverse experiences, influenced by the past and necessary for the spiritual growth of the individual, are gained. Its purpose is fulfilled when these experiences are realized and, like a suit of worn clothing, it is shed. The Self, however, will continue to seek new and appropriate forms, like new garments, to continue its pilgrimage. The purpose of rebirth is the growth of the individual. It provides opportunities for spiritual evolution and development. Since death is a necessary condition for rebirth, it is also understood, in Hinduism, to be a gateway for fresh opportunities. Our own vision is usually confined to a single life experience, and even within that it is often very limited. The boundless past and the unending future are closed to us. We can evaluate the meaning of events and experiences from a very limited perspective. It is a perspective from which the tragic dimension of death impresses us most forcefully. Without denying this tragic element, the Hindu also has to admit that the perspective must be different for the Lord whose vision is unlimited and who is the Lord of both life and death. Where we see end and loss, there will be new beginnings and renewed opportunities. In the Hindu view, the word life is not restricted to describing the span of time between birth and death. Life is a process, and process always implies change. Death and birth are moments in the process of life.

The new physical form, with which the Self identifies after discarding a previous one, is determined mainly by its accumulated tendencies, traits, and desires. A suitable form is sought where these may find fulfillment, even as, in life, we are drawn to an environment where our interests and dispositions may find satisfaction. It is an ancient Hindu custom, therefore, to create around the dying person an atmosphere of spirituality and holiness, so that this may be impressed on the individual's mind.

Earlier, I introduced the Hindu idea of life as a long pilgrimage stretching over many existences. I also said that it is the light of life which makes death intelligible. This discussion on death would not be complete without considering the aim and culmination of the pilgrimage.

While there are some variations in views among the many traditions of Hinduism, we all agree that life is a journey to reality. It is a quest for that which is true and real, that which is free from change and limitations in the midst of an existence, which is so changeful and finite. In Hinduism, that which is real and true, referred to in Sanskrit as *Sat*, is implicitly accepted to have the highest value, and to be the source of all joy. Gandhi was expressing a typical Hindu view when he affirmed that it is more correct to say that Truth is God, than to say that God is Truth. We are all seekers and pilgrims. What distinguishes us is our awareness or lack of awareness that our journey is towards that which is ultimately true. This sacred journey, according to Hinduism, will continue as long as it takes us to discover this final truth of the world and ourselves. As long as we cling to the finite and the changeful and seek comfort and solace in these, our odyssey will be never-ending. *Avidyā*, that is, ignorance, is nothing but our inability to distinguish the true and real from the false and perishable. Ignorance condemns us to frustration and want, since we will never be truly satisfied with the mortal and finite. Freedom, claims Hinduism, lies only in reality. In its attainment lies the fulfillment of our pilgrimage. This is liberation or *mokṣa*, the triumph over death, our true home and destination. The longing for it is captured in the daily Hindu prayer:

> Lead us from untruth to truth
> From ignorance to knowledge
> From death to immortality

Hinduism never encourages the active seeking of death, but emphasizes that we should always be prepared for its inevitability. We must learn to make a journey of love with those whom life has blessed as our companions, but we must also learn to part at the end of the journey. If we have learned to travel well, we will also part well.

Chapter 4

The Spirituality of Action in the Bhagavadgītā

The *Bhagavadgītā*, which, in English, means "the song of the Lord" is undoubtedly the most popular religious text for Hindus throughout the world. This status has been achieved by its own merit and wide appeal, since its official authority is secondary to that of the *Vedas*. In Hinduism, the *Vedas* are regarded as the ultimate source and authority for our knowledge of God. Yet, the *Bhagavadgītā* has irresistibly charmed, stolen, and enshrined itself in the hearts of Hindus everywhere, and is regarded as a guide for moral conduct in the world. In recent times, Mahatma Gandhi expressed the profound Hindu reverence for the *Gītā* as a mother and wrote:

> I lost my earthly mother who gave me birth long ago, but this eternal mother has completely filled her place by my side ever since. She has never changed. She has never failed me. When

> I am in difficulty or distress, I seek refuge in her bosom ....

The *Gītā*, which consists of eighteen chapters, is embedded in the great Hindu epic, the *Mahābhārata*. It is structured in the form of a dialogue between Kṛṣṇa, the Incarnation of God, and Arjuna, His friend and disciple. Since Kṛṣṇa's message is offered as a solution to a shattering moral crisis in Arjuna's life, and also has a relevance for our time, I wish to examine briefly the background and nature of this crisis.

The *Mahābhārata* tells the story of two ancient ruling clans, the Kauravas and Pāṇḍavas. The Pāṇḍavas have been unjustly deprived of their property and wealth by the Kauravas, and the latter turn down countless attempts to negotiate a just settlement. Even the efforts of Kṛṣṇa himself prove futile. The corrupt and selfish Kaurava leader, Duryodhana, refuses to concede the reduced demands of the Pāṇḍavas. The moral issue is a clear one, and war seems inevitable. Arjuna, a leading member of the Pāṇḍava family, chooses Kṛṣṇa, the Lord Incarnate, to be his charioteer. On the day of the battle, he requests Kṛṣṇa to drive his chariot between the two armies, so that he could survey the ranks of his opponents. Arjuna is overwhelmed by what he sees. Many of his former friends, relatives, and even teachers have turned out to support the corrupt Kaurava leader. This confuses the entire moral issue for Arjuna. His desire for victory, power, and wealth melts away, and he loses his will to fight. The material benefits of this war are obvious to Arjuna, but he no longer sees these as good enough reasons for doing battle with his relatives and associates. "Even though they should slay me," he says, "yet I could not wish to slay them, not for dominion over the three worlds, how much less for the earth alone! (1:35)" Arjuna is full of doubts about the spiritual benefit of the war to himself. In fact, as an alternative to fighting, he expresses a preference for the inactive life of a recluse, earning his living by begging. Eventually, Arjuna admits his total confusion and helplessness, and turns to Kṛṣṇa for guidance. "Tell me for certain," he says, "what is good for me. I am your disciple, and I am taking refuge in you.(2:7)"

In Hindu society at the time of the *Bhagavadgītā*, the roles and responsibilities of human beings were very clearly defined. As a *kṣatriya*, that is, a soldier, Arjuna's obligation was to defend his society against injustice. Because this task became personally painful, Arjuna expresses a desire to withdraw from society altogether, and to pursue his spiritual salvation in solitude and inaction.

The manner in which Arjuna formulates his choice, indicates that he sees the pursuit of spiritual freedom, that is, *mokṣa*, as being incompatible with a life of action in society or as providing no justification for it. This was perhaps the prevalent view of his time and it is a view which is still common among many Hindus today. Arjuna speaks of living on alms, and this makes it clear that his image of spirituality is that of the traditional *saṁnyāsin*, that is, the monk who has turned his back on society in order to devote himself exclusively to the pursuit of spiritual knowledge.

The Hindu tradition upholds *mokṣa* as the highest aim of life, and, in expressing a preference for this, Arjuna hoped to win the support of Kṛṣṇa. But even more importantly, he undoubtedly expected Kṛṣṇa to approve of his wish to pursue *mokṣa* by abandoning his responsibilities in society. Spiritual knowledge, he felt, would absolve him from the challenge of action.

Arjuna, however, was to be disappointed. While Kṛṣṇa affirms *mokṣa* to be the ultimate human aim, He does not see it as necessarily justifying the abandonment of action and involvement in the world. The uniqueness and enduring contribution of the *Gītā* to Hinduism is the reconciling and harmonizing of spirituality and action.

Kṛṣṇa clearly challenges the view that the inactive life of the traditional monk is naturally superior and virtuous. There is no natural connection, He argues, between refraining from activity and attaining spiritual freedom. Besides, Kṛṣṇa challenges, what do we mean by inaction? Is such a state at all possible for any human being? Total inaction, He answers, is impossible for a single moment, since action is an inseparable characteristic of existence itself. Even the mere maintenance of bodily life, adds Kṛṣṇa becomes impossible with activity (3:4-8).

Kṛṣṇa's point is that spirituality would be impossible if it depended on the individual being non-active. His suggestion is that even for the *saṁnyāsin*, that is, the monk, some actions are unavoidable. If these actions are not incompatible with *mokṣa*, where, and by what criteria does one draw the limit. The implication of Kṛṣṇa's argument, of course, is that there is no inherent opposition between action in society per se, and spiritual freedom. On the other hand, He does not suggest that actions of all kinds, performed with any motive, are consistent with the aim of spirituality. Kṛṣṇa highly recommends and asserts the superiority of the life of action, but He also carefully and consistently defines the nature of acceptable action. It is to this definition that we must now turn our attention.

When Arjuna saw that the defense of justice would involve him in a struggle against associates, he discovered that he could not be motivated by his desire for wealth and power. He thought that by opting for spiritual freedom (*mokṣa*) he would be relieved of any justification for acting. This conclusion of Arjuna is based on the inference that since *mokṣa* results in an inner fullness, contentment, and freedom from selfish desires, it also removes the motivation for individual action. The important question, however, which Kṛṣṇa raises is whether inner emptiness and self-oriented desires are the only justification for action. In Kṛṣṇa's view, the spiritual fullness and sense of fulfillment which is synonymous with *mokṣa* really provides the opportunity for a newer and higher level of action. Freedom from self-centered desires is not an end in itself. It only provides the freedom to act selflessly for others. Kṛṣṇa refers to this motive for action as *lokasaṅgraha*, that is, action directed to the welfare of others. He upholds it as the highest justification for action.

In seeking to lift us to this vision of action, Kṛṣṇa, the Lord Incarnate, offers Himself as the example, and describes His own motive for action in the world. "As the Lord," Kṛṣṇa says, "there is nothing personal for Me to gain or accomplish through action. Yet," he adds, "I will continue to ceaselessly act in order to set the right example, and for the preservation of the world. (3:22-24)"

In the vision of Kṛṣṇa, therefore, the spiritual freedom which Arjuna desires does not release one from social responsibilities. On the contrary, it only makes these responsibilities more obvious and provides a richer justification for social involvement. At every level, according to Kṛṣṇa, the world needs the example of unselfish spirituality in action. The responsibility to provide this example rests with the human being who has attained *mokṣa.* The enthusiasm of such a person in working for the welfare of others, says Kṛṣṇa, should equal that of the selfish individual feverishly pursuing personal desires.

Consistent with His preference for the active life which is inspired by spiritual knowledge, Kṛṣṇa offers a revolutionary definition of renunciation. In traditional Hinduism, renunciation consisted of a literal abandonment of relationships and responsibilities. Kṛṣṇa, however, emphasizes the inward attitude. Renunciation, he affirms, is the overcoming of the selfish motive in action. It is the ability to act selflessly without attachment to personal rewards.

Arjuna saw two alternatives. He could either act in society for personal ends, or withdraw from social involvement to pursue *mokṣa* in relative isolation. For Kṛṣṇa, however, this was not the real choice. The human being could continue to act selfishly through spiritual ignorance. Alternatively, one could, through the fullness and freedom of *mokṣa* act joyously for the welfare of others. Our actions can imprison us; but they can also be the song of our freedom. This is the challenge to us of the *Bhagavadgītā*, the song of the Lord.

Chapter 5

A Hindu Looks at Jesus

Growing up in Trinidad, a small Caribbean island of ethnic, cultural, and religious pluralism, it seems inevitable that I should know of Jesus from a very young age. I can easily recall participating in nativity plays at Christmas time in nursery school. As young boys, we used to attend the local Sunday School for the fun of it. In fact, the church was located next to the house in which we lived at that time. I can still vividly remember how elated I felt when I answered what seemed to be an incredibly difficult question. This concerned the length of time Joseph knocked on the innkeeper's door the night Jesus was born. The various answers kept coming for a long time. Some of the answers attempted to quantify the number of knocks, some sought to fix a specific length of time. Suddenly, without thinking about it, I yelled, 'until the door was opened,' and it was a kind of triumph. I think we were particularly attracted by and enjoyed the quiz at the end of each class.

Christian missionaries regularly called at our home to

talk and to distribute literature. At Easter time most of the cinemas showed films on the life of Jesus, and we invariably went to one of these. In Trinidad there is the custom, on Good Friday, of building a hideous replica of Judas. This is displayed at the roadside, and at the end of the day it is thrashed and burnt. We would use the soft trunk of the banana plant to construct the body, fix branches into it for arms and legs, and stuff the clothing with dried banana leaves. It was really a time of great excitement for us.

In view of the fact that I came from an orthodox Hindu family, and both my grandfathers were Hindu priests, our participation in these various activities appears quite strange. In Trinidad, however, the boundaries of participation in each other's major religious festivals and celebrations are not rigid, and it is quite fair to say that religious communities are well acquainted with each other's major symbols, figures, and celebrations.

I received my secondary education at a Presbyterian college founded by Canadian missionaries, and here again there were many opportunities to hear of Jesus. It was at this time that I started seriously to read literature on Hinduism. I turned particularly to the voluminous works of the Hindu monk, Swami Vivekandanda, and here, as in other writers, the references to Jesus were many. Paradoxically, my interest in Jesus was encouraged and deepened by Hindu writers. The interest of major Hindu figures of the nineteenth and twentieth centuries in Jesus also prompted me to read the New Testament.

From the perspective and background of my own Hindu tradition, I did not find it difficult to identify with the figure of Jesus. In fact, I found him positively attractive. Deeply attracted as I was at that time by the ideal of the Hindu *saṁnyāsin* (monk), I was able immediately to see in Jesus many of the qualities of this ideal. Here was a wandering spiritual teacher without home or possessions, fired by the true spirit of renunciation (*vairāgya*). Here also was one who spoke with authority about the limitations and futility of the life which was spent solely in the selfish accumulation of wealth (*artha*) and transitory sense enjoyment (*kāma*). Here also was one who taught about 'the kingdom of heaven within,' and emphasized that there was a meaning and significance to life, and that it was possible on the basis of this to live in freedom, fullness, and peace. I found that the symbols and images, the parables and examples used by Jesus in talking about the spiritual life were not entirely different from those employed in some Hindu texts. His emphasis on the primacy and fundamental nature of the spiritual life echoed for me the concern in the *Upaniṣads* with spiritual knowledge (*jñāna*) as the prerequisite to the full life.

> When men shall roll up space
> As though it were a piece of leather,
> Then will there be an end of sorrow
> For him who knew not God.
> *Śvetāśvatara Upaniṣad* 6.16

What, therefore, initially attracted me in the personality of Jesus is the embodiment in him of what I considered to be, from my Hindu viewpoint, the ideals and values of the authentic spiritual life. This dimension of Jesus has always continued to have a meaning and appeal for me. From my own very limited perspective of Christianity, I think that this primary aspect of the personality of Christ is not always sufficiently emphasized in presenting him. I imagine that it will always be difficult to present one who cared so little for the comforts and possessions which are usually the focus of our energies and aspirations, and whose life was so totally a reflection of its center in a higher reality. As human beings, we have mastered the art of both subtly and nakedly using our respective spiritual traditions and ideals to mask and serve our own insatiable ego-centered ambitions. It seems hopeless when that which is meant to free us from the constraints of the ego becomes the servant of its narrow interests. But perhaps in its concern to stress the uniqueness and originality of Jesus, Christianity has ignored some of the identities in the definition of the spiritual life which Jesus shares with the tradition of Hinduism. I think that it is the ready perception of these identities, however, which initially attracted outstanding Hindus like Ram Mohun Roy, Keshub Chandra Sen, Vivekananda and Gandhi to Jesus. The Hindu who is steeped in the values of his own tradition feels a natural affinity for the self-evident and radiant spirituality of Jesus, and wishes in the enthusiasm of this recognition to welcome him into his home.

Along with what I can only weakly describe as an authentic and self-manifesting spirituality, there is another dimension of the character of Jesus which I find meaningful and appealing. I would add that this dimension has become more significant and apparent to me in recent times. In Hinduism we are very familiar with the idea that genuine spiritual knowledge cannot be imparted without an appropriate preparedness, readiness, and growth on the part of the receiver. In our quest for spiritual knowledge, newer and deeper dimensions of the same message are unfolded as we ourselves grow inwardly, and perhaps this is the case here. The dimension of Jesus' character to which I am referring is his outstanding demonstration of what genuine spirituality means in the process of actually living in the world. I think that he has provided some of the most concrete and finest examples of practical spirituality, or what the spiritual life means when it is translated into human relationships. In his life he has given us some of the fullest instances of the fruits of the spiritual life in action. I find no difficulty, as a Hindu, in deriving guidance and inspiration from these, since I think that any authentic spirituality cannot but translate itself into this mode of relating, not only to human beings, but to all life.

In the context of this practical spirituality, I think, in particular, of the many examples of his spontaneous and limitless compassion. I think of his unconditional love, tenderness, and humility. I think also of his capacity for suffering and self-sacrifice, and his effortless forgiving. I have often reflected on the source of that boundless compassion which, even when life itself is being cruelly and painfully snatched away, choicelessly forgives. From what unfathomable depths of love such words flowed ... and how petty, trifling, and narrow we seem in the light of its splendor. If authentic spirituality is to bear any fruit, there is no doubt that it must consist of the qualities which were reflected in Jesus' relationships. The source of a spirituality which is not characterized by an active compassion, unconditional love, gentleness, humility, self-sacrifice, and non-retribution must always be suspect and questionable.

I find that Jesus' emphasis on a living spirituality which informs and pervades all our relationships and even our smallest actions to be very meaningful. The practical spirituality of Jesus is one of the important sources which has acted as a stimulus to the further exploration of my own tradition. I have felt the necessity to ask more urgently of my own tradition, its implications for life in society. I feel the importance of trying to draw out from it the meaning of its vision when converted into the terms of daily living and the problems of human beings in societies. Any worthy claim about the nature of ultimate reality must also be realized in terms of values and attitudes which contribute to the resolving of the fundamental conflicts and problems of our life in the world, and enable us to live peacefully and joyfully.

On the basis of reflecting in this direction on my own tradition, I feel very strongly that the fruits of Hindu spirituality, in terms of the attitudes and values which should guide our human relationships, coincide with those exemplified in the life of Jesus. At the same time, I think that there is a need for contemporary Hinduism to seek more urgently to gather and emphasize the practical implications in society of its profound philosophical views about the nature of ultimate reality. Hinduism has evinced a great and no doubt legitimate concern with metaphysics, especially in those traditions which emphasize the importance of knowledge (*jñāna*) and the means of attaining spiritual freedom (*mokṣa*). This concern, however, always needs the corrective balance provided by a stress on its significance for our human relationships and our life in society. This stress is again needed in contemporary Hinduism if it is to make its own vital and unique contribution, along with other religious traditions, to resolving the complex problems of our modern world.

In the *Upaniṣads*, for example, the central concern is the attainment of *mokṣa*. Moral and ethical values are presumed and implied rather than directly discussed. *Mokṣa*, however, as an end which involves a certain vision of ourselves and the world, has profound implications for the transformation of our relationships, and the *Upaniṣads* entrust us with the task of seeking out this fruit and creatively applying it in our lives. The actual and vivid examples of Jesus, and my contact with his followers, have intensified my awareness of the necessity and importance of this. This is not to suggest, however, that such values are never directly discussed. The *Bṛhadāraṇyaka Upaniṣad* 5.2.1-3, for example, enjoins upon us the values of self-restraint (*dama*), giving (*dāna*), and compassion. In a text like the *Bhagavadgītā*, the references are more direct. Among the values mentioned there, both as a means to the authentic spiritual life and as the fruits of this life, are compassion (*karuṇā*), humility (*amānitvam*), sharing (*dāna*), gentleness (*mārdavaṁ*), forgiveness (*kṣamā*), modesty (*hrī*), harmlessness (*ahiṁsā*), purity (*śaucam*), fearlessness (*abhayaṁ*), patience (*kṣānti*), serenity (*śānti*), and freedom from egoism (*nirahaṁkāra*)—[12.13-19; 13.7-11; 16.1-3]. These are undoubtedly among the important values emphasized and exemplified in the life of Jesus.

This coincidence in the values of the authentic spiritual life is an area for further mutual exploration between our respective traditions, and a basis on which our traditions can act together. We need to understand more closely how we interpret these values and the ways in which they ought to be reflected in our life in the world. As a Hindu, one has to resist the inclination to see and interpret Jesus in the categories of Hinduism. This approach was very common in the nineteenth and early twentieth centuries and it is not unusual today. The attempt is often made to see his life and teachings in the categories of the Hindu tradition of *advaita* (non-dualism). This, however, is only possible through a very selective use of the records of his sayings, and the dismissal of the way in which he has been traditionally understood by most Christians. It is an approach which claims to place little importance on dogma and doctrine, and, therefore, dismisses the significance of differences in this sphere. In reality, however, such differences must be acknowledged. Dismissing them in sweeping generalizations does not contribute much to the process of mutual understanding.

At the other end, however, we can intensify the emphasis on our differences and overlook or explain away all coincidences. To many who are acquainted with both traditions, the identities which are argued for here may appear to be insignificantly obvious. But a sharing between two traditions about the cardinal values which constitute the spiritual life, and which should light up our conduct in the world, can never be without significance. These are not the peripheral concerns of any religion, but may be said to lie at the very heart of their meaning.

There remains the challenging and compelling fact that on the basis of very different 'readings,' 'interpretations,' or 'responses' to ultimate reality and the human predicament, there is a certain vital coincidence about the values of authentic spirituality. This cannot but hold some meaning, and the suggestions and implications of this meaning will have to be considered by our traditions individually and jointly. Here I can only think of a few of the innumerable questions. Does it mean that there are different ways of 'reading' the same reality, and that our traditions are employing one or the other of these standpoints? Are these standpoints incompatible, and, if so, where does this incompatibility lie? Can different standpoints in some way complement each other? And does it imply that all our categories and standpoints are in some way limited and partial, and that the reality we are 'reading' ultimately transcends them all?

Bibliography

WORKS CITED

Chatterjee, S. *The Fundamentals of Hinduism.* Calcutta: University of Calcutta, 1970.

Eck, D. *Darśan: Seeing the Divine Image in India.* Pennsylvania: Anima Books, 1985.

Radhakrishnan, S. *The Hindu View of Life.* London: Unwin Paperbacks, 1980.

Waghorne, J. P. and Cutler N., eds. *Gods of Flesh/Gods of Stone.* Pennsylvania: Anima Publications, 1985.

FURTHER READING

Bhagavadgītā, S. Radhakrishnan, trans. London: Allen and Unwin, 1956.

Chatterjee, S. and Datta, D. M. *An Introduction to Indian Philosophy.* Calcutta: University of Calcutta, 1968.

Klostermaier, K. K. *A Survey of Hinduism.* New York: State University of New York Press, 1989.

Mahadevan, T. M. P. *Outlines of Hinduism.* Bombay: Chetna, 1960.

Organ, T. W. *The Hindu Quest for the Perfection of Man.* Ohio: Ohio University Press, 1970.

Rambachan, Anantanand. *Accomplishing the Accomplished: The Vedas as a Source of Valid Knowledge in Śaṅkara.* Honolulu: University of Hawaii Press, 1991.

Sarma, D. S. *Hinduism Through the Ages*, rev. ed. Bombay: Bharatiya Vidya Bhavan, 1958.

____. *A Primer of Hinduism.* Madras: Sri Ramakrishna Math, 1984.

Satprakashananda, Swami. *The Goal and the Way.* St. Louis: The Vedanta Society of St. Louis, 1977.

Sharma, S. *A Critical Survey of Indian Philosophy.* Delhi: Motilal Banarsidass, 1976.

Index